Lessons in The Breath

Stephanie Van Horn

Lessons in The Breath

Two Muses Press, Portland, OR 97202

© 2020 by Stephanie Van Horn

All rights reserved. Published by Two Muses Press. No part of this publication may be reproduced or distributed in any form or by any means, or stored in a database or retrieval system, without the prior written permission of the publisher.

Cover design by Doug Hunt @ doughuntart.com.

Proofreading and interior book design provided by Indigo: Editing, Design, and More:

- Proofreader: Ali Shaw
- Interior book design: Vinnie Kinsella

www.indigoediting.com

ISBN: 978-0-578-77802-0

For my nephews, Isaac and Ian

What is it to cease breathing,
but to free the breath
from its restless tides,
that it may rise and expand
and seek God unencumbered?

—Kahlil Gibran, *The Prophet*

Contents

I. *Survivor*

Return 3
Sufficiency 5
Childhood 7
The Good Child 8
Dream Sonnets: Crossing Over 10
The Empty Village 11
Churchgoing: The Annual Visit 12
Reflection: The Annual Visit 14
Weather People 16
A Country and Western Song 18
As My Father Turns Eighty 19
That Winter 21
Survivor 22
Accomplice 24
My Mother's Moving Man 25
Mother-Daughter Ghazal 26
My Mother Thinks of the Afterlife 28
Life Count 29
Daylight Savings Time 30

II. *This Random World*

Yes 33
Safety 34
Kathmandu Photograph 36
Exploring the Dark 38
Alaska Autumn 40
Spring Manual 42
Raids on Afghanistan 43
It Could Have Been 1825 44
For an 8 a.m. Class in Sentence Fundamentals 46

My 8 a.m. Class Admits to Tears	48
Corrida	50
Blue Linoleum	53
Amazons	54
For Donald	56
Travelers	58
Teotitlán del Valle	60
Descent	62
Oaxaca Journal	63
Amina from Kashmir	65
Yugoslavia	66
Woman at the Window	67

III. *Family Tree*

Arithmetic	75
Letter to Alaska	77
After the Visit	78
Farm Women	79
Fever—1924	82
Two Across	83
In Her Kitchen	84
My Aunt Speaks	85
Postcard: Family Reunion 1905, Nebraska	86
Gospel According to Phoebe	88
Riding Lesson	89
Surface and Strata	91
First Cousins	93

IV. *Stopping Time*

Stopping Time	97
Balancing, Bowing	98
Storage System	99
Nocturne	100
Beauty	101
Luck at the El Gato	102

The Lump	103
One Season Goes	104
The First Year Married	105
The Quarrel	106
Dream Sonnet	107
This Year	108
This Poem	110
Report from the Bee Tree	111

V. *Rink Creek Journal*

Our First Words Each Day	115
What Do I Know?	116
Matins	117
The Wheel	119
In the Lane	120
Obedience	122
Abandoned	123
The Green World	124
January	125
Hands	126
K Country	128
Flood Summer	129
The Month of Forest Fires	130
Black Bear	132
Loss	133
Discovery	135
Past Forty	136
The Breathing Lesson	138
Acknowledgments	141
Biography	143

I
Survivor

Return

From where I stand now,
just a visitor to a birthplace,
the past is concealed.
The faded red of the fallen barn
no longer gleams, the shattered gates
no longer hold the future safe for market.
Sumac chokes my father's fields,
and on the hillside
hides the creamery station
where once the milk trains
sighed and stopped and woke me.
There too the past is lost.
From this gaunt farmhouse,
I watch summer rain
wash coal to dust
between the rusting rails,
forty summers washed away
since I once stood
where I stand now,
breathing mist on a broken pane.
I learned to count on boxcars,
numbering the Burlington Northern,
the Rock Island line,
schooled myself in railroad colors,
Santa Fe orange, Baltimore green,
then learned directions,
north and south, east and west,
all of my trains endlessly leaving.
I came to mourn the absent farm.
From where I stand now,

between two gravestones,
railroad, land,
I cannot choose.
I walk the fields,
survivor, grieving
for the friendship
of the last train whistle.

Sufficiency

Perhaps it's because of toys
that I remember childhood as happy.
My green steel tractor not much like my father's
but still good at work around the metal barn
assembled by my father Christmas Eve, tab A, tab B,
his temper uncertain especially around holidays.
Next morning he seemed cheerful enough,
gave me bullet casings, .22 and 30 aught 6,
to fence the farmhouse made of Lincoln Logs,
a windmill of tinker toys, happy farmer, jolly wife,
a dog much like my border collie, tail
in a perpetual wag, immortal plastic chickens,
cows, sheep, a brown horse ready
for Roy and Dale adventures
in some canyon land west of New Jersey.

My dolls, sometimes my children, who wet
and rolled their eyes alarmingly
when carried naked by one leg,
sometimes were city friends just visiting
in one high heel and an evening dress
made by my aunt Carrie. They
sipped from a Sears, Roebuck tea set
in the arched room under the yellow forsythia bush,
napped together in a hand-me-down wooden crib,
jostling for space with stuffed animals,
covered with my mother's scarves and a kitchen towel.
Much rearrangement of lives and stories
as their eyes and mine opened and shut.

Beyond the gray, anxious house, the playground farm.
The barn with kittens born among the hay bales
before the scraggy mother moved them safely on,
before my father drowned them in the pond.
Day after day I crossed the fields, dipped from the brook,
water slipped through my busy hands.
I rode my stubborn pony, fed my mother's goats,
drank milk fresh from my father's cows,
chased lightning bugs until
my father took me up the stairs,
stories about myself that were always happy.
I slept tight, no bedbugs to bite.
Sufficient, enough of everything they had.

Childhood

I used to hide, run blind,
between the lines of sheets,
my parents' sheets and mine.
My mother's hands rubbed the silver washboard,
my father's pants hung on their frame.
The branch from our woods
held up the rope
with shirts and skirts,
towels and gowns.
The pulley sent us out
to sun and breeze
and brought us back again,
knew where we were going,
our cleansed, our spotless selves.
And I ran blind.

The Good Child

There was a child in her father's house one evening,
an unpainted, breakable farmhouse,
black glass staring windows, harsh-shouldered eaves,
a child sitting like every other evening,
a warrior's circle of blocks, dolls, and books,
outside which her father's armies pace away their losses,
where her mother weeps an arrowed fog
that nearly covers the child.

Unless
she builds a castle
and peoples it,
dresses the doll just so,
choosing this ribbon, that hat.
Her own brown shoes, her father calls
"sensible."

Unless she bends over a book,
pulls flannel fantasies over her
against cold lamplight
where her father's drumming fingers
advance and fall, advance and fall,
nowhere to go but a wooden chair arm.

Were she better fed, were there not sieges
where her parents hoard praise,
where the salt of stubbornness
is unknown to her, she might
turn her blocks to bombs,
remind them of her citizenship.

Instead, she sets the wooden triangle on an arch,
the entrance to her city, moves her arm
just enough for this forayed action,
as one ventures a few fingers toward large dogs,
moves silently, which pleases the parents.
The pages of a book make little sound as well.
Some days her voice seems as rusty as the well pump.

It is a good flannel woven here.
When her father shouts, shakes her, slams
out into the rain, when her mother
comforts herself with committees,
she builds a small stockade of her father's bullet casings
where a brown plastic horse and its foal
can safely graze.

Dream Sonnets: Crossing Over

The child has no control. When the parent
leads, she follows, the world frontiers, her freedom gone.
That California summer, a girl twelve bent
on being five or thirty, her father home
from the mental ward, silent, edgy. Change
shuddered in the hottest air she'd felt.
Her aunts drive them daily to strange
houses. She sulks, calls her brother "brat,"
counts sad rhymes on her fingers, clair-
voyant of the next act, the green home farm
auctioned for this heat, her father's life. Weeps more,
her back seat weight, her rhymes all useless charms.
I often dream of moves, still parents' pawn,
the frightened child. Last night I woke lost again.

The Empty Village

What can a street say to the girl who once made it her ocean,
voyaged from shoemaker to the hardware store?
House after house is moored and shuttered,
I can say their names still—Bailey, Morrow, Muller, Brown.
An hour's walk then felt like years gone,
the traveler's trick already known,
the remnants of a journey's change.
The mind takes time's crumpled sail, furls it.
Takes the crumpled laundry of summer hours,
irons them creaseless, folds the past, loses nothing.
The world of matter lets it all go.
Even milkweed floating in the August air—
the cold wind of winter propels its fall.

Churchgoing: The Annual Visit

I don't know whether religion is what I need.
Most days when I walk these back roads,
the word *God* is a locked gate. I don't climb over.
Today hymn after hymn follows me,
the rasp of familiar stones, my feet
filling hollows they've known before.

I go to church here.
Between offertory and benediction
my sure memory for creeds
and the names of old neighbors
misleads me. I want to believe.
I want to join this congregation,
today pledged to a red-haired baby
who shines with baptismal water,
snowbound in white crochet.
I want to run these roads
and still say "God" on an easy breath.

Lately I don't ask much of myself,
go here, go there, come home to this church,
recite with false conviction what my father believes,
my voice carrying above my mother's whisper,
carrying the child I once was,
crowned before this congregation too
with clear spring water.

The minister asks our promise.
Memory offers me a covenant.
Each breath released searches
the abandoned pastures beside me.
Each breath returned forgives me:
I have not answered my catechism's last question.
I have this much faith—the next breath
will rise without being called.

Reflection: The Annual Visit

The flesh under my arms
has become webbed
has the crease and quiver
of fallen bread dough
like yours.

All week
light daughter, dark mother
we have looked at each other
across an oak table
the same cold coffee forgotten,
reading British novels, the same map
worn on forehead, eyelid.
Tugging at our graying hair.

Like a story problem
we are a mathematics
of passing years,
we have become
the same age.
Old women,
women getting
old.

Do you remember
the year of mother/daughter dresses,
how unlike we were?
I only say this
seeing your reflection in the bus window
as we wave
goodbye.

Weather People

I call the old farmer once a month to talk weather,
no "Daughter, I love you," no "Father dear,"
just rain gauges, windchill, morning highs and lows.
We watch for the cusps of change
when the barometer runs away with itself,
when it's worth stepping outside to watch the sky.
Each time we move, we buy
that country's words for weather—
I have fifty words for northwest rain,
he left speechless California,
speaks again his native tongue,
"thunder, blizzard, autumn, autumn."

Sometimes we ride high on weather balloons,
five days of sun for me, a summer when breezes
pollinate his sweet corn, when he sleeps nights.
I remember springs there when golden light
scissored the leaves of hundred-year-old maples,
viridian green, heart shapes lifting from the wind's adrenaline.
He doesn't tell me that. He says, "Cool nights,
enough rain, east wind."

"Hello, Father. I am a mist that glitters on the dog's black coat
as we walk to the mailbox. I am a cloudy day,
perhaps sun breaking through soon."

"Hello, Daughter. I am still, maybe a bad storm coming in.
Last week I was east wind and an argument of hard rain.
But tomorrow, tomorrow, perhaps a fine day,
blue as our Dutch eyes, sharp as our cheekbones,
sunlit as our hair."

My husband asks, "What's in the letter?"
I reply, "Just news about the weather."

A Country and Western Song

A father and daughter are lost
on a country road, lost
in a neighbor's living room,
addicted to the cold, cold heart,
the white-hat heroin of Hank Williams,
his face stained gray in the hemisphere
of the '50s Philco, someone lost
on a country road calling from Nashville.
Something in the trip and fall, lost and found
of his high notes rescues them.

Just after the war, couples square their sets,
Saturday nights allemande to the father's baritone.
The daughter swims, still sacked in his scrotum,
in time with the anvil guitar.
Just back from the mental hospital,
he sells the guitar. Ask him
and he has forgotten the war,
the roads to North Africa and Germany
blown up by electroshock.

By the time she is a woman, he is a bee in amber,
beating his wings to selected songs.
She brings him a Walkman. The tapes
of his old familiar lie beside him singing—
Saturday nights he sang, "Ol' Kaw-liga,"
in the car beside her, sang,
"We'll go honky-tonking honey baby,"
sang to her, all the way home.

As My Father Turns Eighty

The best days, when I went with him
on paths across the still heat of spring pastures,
were my watercolor paint box green and yellow,
the gleam of the juice glass holding water
that I dip into to remember.
The source of it all, the brook,
never got lost from its muddy brown arms,
and after we safely crossed over, my father
would take the pocket knife he always
kept by him, cut the shoots that grew
below white birch trees
and say, "Here, chew."

The bark slipped between my teeth,
the tender wood released its bright taste.
My grandfather had taught him this, he said.

I could hardly see the store, its shelves,
for the dust and dazzle still in my eyes
from looking hard down the road as he did
through the window of the pickup in case
of box turtles or potholes or danger or
any disturbance to us, those long days,
the hay dust in the red creases
of my father's neck.

From the square red cooler, he gave me
a thick small bottle spring brook dripping wet,
clear and brown, said, "Here, taste."

Birch beer is gone now from the country stores
where we once stood quietly together,
listening I think to brooks beside white birches
that grow so close to each other.

That Winter

Darkness outside, then within
as I touch the light switches one last time—
a sleepy eyelid, the house closes down.
The parakeets, blue-feathered eggs, huddle together.
I too will nest in darkness while, across three time zones,
my mother has been asleep for hours.
Novocain soothes her where the radiation burns.
My father drowses in his hospital bed,
tubes of oxygen, barbiturates, antibiotics
lace him into sleep, all of us
shadowed and quiet,
separate, together.

Since reading a magazine of beautiful homes today
because it was the furthest thing from my parents' lives,
I've wanted the plates I saw there.
Lucent, a gleam I can no more touch
than the flames in the woodstove.
Transparent as worn linen, petals
of winter's paperwhites.
Old skin. The gold rims
chipped with an SOS that tonight
I pretend not to understand.

Survivor

Sweating, breathless against
the summer heat and mothballs
of my father's closet, I fill

eight plastic lawn and garden sacks with his clothing.
Downstairs my brother calls insurance companies,
and my mother lists the banks.

Each night she falls asleep
in her dead husband's recliner
with the illusion of something finally done.

Really, nothing is as easy
as it might seem to his firefly ghost
in darkness watching us,

the three survivors moving to and fro
in the lighted house they took him from,
zipped in the sterile body bag.

It is stay, no, let them go—
his well-shined shoes, the shirt from L.L.Bean
I gave him on last year's birthday.

I keep the vest from his wedding suit,
but the long outgrown woolen pants and jacket
spill like leaves from the black sacks,

weights that fill his little car that I park
by the bright-blue dumpster labeled AMVETS,
shaded by trees in the supermarket lot.

At the last moment, I drop his glasses
into my briefcase, safe from charity,
wonder if one more task will set me free.

Accomplice

Sleep now, old gun,
the pond's green your blanket,
the shadows of swans dreams above you,
the cattail roots, bedroom walls.
Rust, return, element of earth,
not enough of you remaining
to harm again.
I will not forget you,
how like all tools,
you were
honest in yourself,
obedient to each hand.
How, after the last explosion,
the old man, frightened
of the next years,
fell, not waiting to see dawn
fill the window under the eaves.
You were his last companion.
And then alone.

My brother's arm arches,
I say, "Yes," and you are laid
into a bed of ripples.
Better that you sleep there.
Better that water bathe you,
fire leave you, earth receive you,
air be free of the bullet's sound.

My Mother's Moving Man

Makes me glad I'm from New Jersey,
easy to match my vowels to his
when he warns about the price of storage units,
when we talk about his mother and mine.
"A real nice lady, your mother."

She has never told me more
than I wanted to know
about finding
my father and the gun,
but I don't want her
to look back as we drive away,
don't want her to see his ghost
waving goodbye from the window
that might have been his last view.

Last night I watched again
the *Challenger* flame its way
to Christa McAuliffe's last view
of all my mother was born to—
New Jersey, the Earth, Solar System.
To do: check storage unit prices, clean
the bedroom closet, give the mailman
my mother's new address.
My father dwells now
in other mansions.

Mother-Daughter Ghazal

There, her morning rounds, brush out gray hair and make the bed,
let one more dozing night push open morning's gate. Thoughts catch at nothing.

Here, gray mist that brushes fence and garden gate, flocks of small birds scatter.
The cat on morning rounds leaps at shadows, catches nothing, waits.

She waits for breakfast, charts her genealogy, three lamps lit like flames
against shadows and her fading eyes. Names flock, then scatter.

Before breakfast I weed old roses, genealogies, name after name, Harison's Yellow,
great-grandmother's remnant, petals like stars a child draws, thorns that bite.

Slow flocks of faded remnants, she and her neighbors flow to breakfast—
in child's bites she chews their names, spills water from her trembling hands.

The rainbird spills water to the dry rose garden. This west coast summer
nothing can grow unless clouds fill slow flocks, underground springs appear.

She spills east coast letters across her desk, fences stories safe in charts, then one day
tells me she's forgetting names, dates, births, deaths, her springs gone underground.

We hold that silent stone in our trembling hands, our knotted knuckles mirrors,
what gate can fence off fog, clouds, slow-spilling rain, tonight three stars flame

On yellow petals dropped like stones before the rain, like names that brush
our dreams in misted flocks, catching nothing, scattered, gone, a child's art.

My Mother Thinks of the Afterlife

In the afterlife we might
sit around picnic tables
exchanging recipes,
reminding each other
how dusty the road
to the reunion was.
Men will play horseshoes,
children will swim
with cousins never met before.
Saint Peter has written
a butcher-paper family tree.
We'll be there for eternity,
tasting Mildred's chicken loaf
Cousin Nellie's chocolate cake,
remembering Aunt Fanny's Sunday hat.
The photographer always comes at noon.

Curling together under car robes at evening,
amazed by love and fireworks,
how bad would that be?

Life Count

For Grace Hunt Van Horn

Lately she has spasms under her breastbone,
counts her pulse frequently. Old hymns
flutter from her throat as unbidden
as migrating birds.

Possessions fill undusted corners,
nest in her thoughts,
so many threads and twigs.
Anxious for the fate of objects sent
into the world brown-paper wrapped,
she asks her children, "Do you
still have my quilt, do you
wear grandmother's ring?"

In her last kitchen, she tallies
visitors to her bird feeders, makes
a life count, wonders
which secret lures the cardinals,
the orioles, back to her each year.

Daylight Savings Time

The time changed yesterday.
How quickly the day disappears,
lost to late sleep and how it felt
sending twenty-six letters to friends and family
six weeks after my mother's death,
telling that truth to paper,
to envelope, to stamp, to distance.
Emptying her apartment,
I emptied too, leaving room
for more tears. I had thought
grief was gone. Its return
surprised me with its bruising.

I walk the dog. I clean the house.
I wash my hair and wear old jeans.
I live between being and knowing.
How I knew which lotion would slip
her wedding ring off,
her skin with no pulse now,
gone beyond measurements of time.

I. She. All memory now.
Her shadow, a child left behind,
learning to tell time again.

II
This Random World

Yes

I didn't know I loved the smaller sounds,
summer cicadas, their high sweetness,
the occasional shower of birds chirping
when traffic quiets, permits their pitch to climb the scale,
the smaller scale discovered in the world's undergrowth,
what is precious, gesturing wildly to be remembered—
until last week when three old men told me stories about
    their dogs.
Two had words I recognized, could see listed in bold letters
as we spoke—*cocker spaniel*, *trick*, *after the war*.
I listened with better attention to the wordless one
whose stroke had left him speech in shadows, intonations.
I had to believe it was a good story.
I had to nod and murmur in exactly the right places.
I was stepping stones, he the bright river.
I heard some dog bark softly. I loved its toes clicking
on the kitchen floor. My friend heard all the small sounds
he used to say, "Come, puppy, down," and what I really heard
was enough to be going on with, to say "Yes, yes" to.
I love the shapelessness of the world, its constant discovery
of uncharted rhythms, accidents in iambic pentameter,
how it speaks when there is absence,
the panting of long-dead dogs, my old men and me,
our jingles and zippers, maybe a last breath,
while in the shadows spring peepers become bullfrogs,
and cicadas and finches direct the traffic of our waning lives.

Safety

Today at my deck feeder
three common ground doves waddle
like my grandmother did
in her feed-sack apron.

I am eating cold meat loaf
and wearing denim,
we are
common as dirt,
nothing highfalutin.
The highfalutin word
quotidian
comes to mind.

I want to play
some Hank Williams,
a simple blues.
Any angels stopping by
—and it feels as if one might—
will be of an order
less immense and terrifying
than the seraphim.

Some other day
for epiphany, the rapture.
Today, in profusion and argument,
small brown birds, ordinary
and nameless,
empty the feeder.

Fed and safe,
in this random world.

Kathmandu Photograph

As the saris hung above me blow
rose and yellow shadows on this page,
color becomes one layer taken to itself by the world.
Yet those tubes emptying onto
the blank surface matter less
than how today the air
holds its breath, becomes an earthquake
as the pages turn, more quickly than
the photographer beyond me moves
through the space sculpted around his finger.

Look through the picture's transparency,
turn to the negative instead—
the space where the dog beside me stares
will still be a long gaze surrounding his body.
The three saris floating are under such pressure
that the alley is scented in an offering
of petals and hennaed dust.
Look at what I am not, the space around me,
until figure-ground confusion fills your eye.
The eye wanders a landscape,
and no object is more important
than the space it speaks to.
There is a landscape around a bird's body,
there are magnetic currents speaking
to its feathers as it flies.

The *I* moves back and forth across the letter.
Expectation attaches itself—
detached, is just information about the heart.

I know what I am and what I am not
for this momentary, frozen frame.
I read my letter between the lines.

.

Exploring the Dark

What dignifies the hand in its slow passage
down another's skin?
The space between surfaces,
air that disappears during the touch,
dies away, returns happier,
as on the exhale the breath
becomes another substance.

The mystery of dissolving distances.
The distant runner growing larger.
The child size of the map after a cross-country flight.
Bringing water across the lips
until it joins water already part of the body,
sweat between two lovers' bodies
returning to the lips again.

On the bus to Michoacán
my husband and a man who sells children's clothing
talk of Buddhism—soon there is no moment
when their languages have not grown together.
I sleep in the field their voices make for me.
We come closer to something,
if only to explain today's tilt of the world
to each other.

The pilgrim's palm turns
from supplication to transcendence,
all because the light that separates two bodies
goes out, slowly, as if a dimmer switch revolves
during the progress of each embrace,
any handshake, touch, the close fit
of darkness near at hand.

Alaska Autumn

We become shortsighted as the days close in,
could overlook the necessary,
see less in careful measured light.
Incandescent aspens barricade the hillside,
Firelight of willow branches cannot reverse
the roll down from the Brooks Range.
Like specters just in view,
the dark months wait.

The clouds, snow descending,
engulf the Dall sheep.
They cluster small,
white approaching white,
then escape the eye.
We draw in, stack wood close,
carry winter chores before us
in eye-obscuring stacks,
await the dark months.

This morning, the air outside sharpened.
We move, cold mercury, slow through brief light.
The marmots preen their freshened weight of fur,
pikas whistle in stacks of winter grass.
Red tundra, brown ranges,
gray talus rockfall.
Alaska forget-me-not,
the last blue sky.

This is the season to wander,
our eyes wander,
before snow binds us
to a lonely point of view.
It is a victory over the shuttered days,
the blinded months, to carry memory
into winter.

Spring Manual

"Heel in the rose," the package says,
directions for each action,
even the simplest filling
of the world with parts of itself.
Mix compost, peat moss,
original dirt kept like a favorite jacket.
Even the wind follows directions,
north changing to south.

Sit with me.
At this angle of light,
we have run out of winter.
The empty jar gleams.
Teaching the neighbor's girl colors,
matching her eyes and crocus,
butter and daffodil,
copper pot, caterpillar,
we search daily
for more instruction—
simple words,
spring.

Raids on Afghanistan
October 8, 2001

What I was forgetting was autumn's explosions,
how I could be turned to darkness
among leaf piles and resurrected,
the child leaping so high and free,
the sunlight shrapnel and splinters
bombed out of autumn's sky.
The garden fills with bodies—
pumpkins upended, blood-red tomatoes.
In another autumn, I would have other words.
This year I have a world rocked in a porch swing
and I am gathering all I might forget.

It Could Have Been 1825

"It was snowing and we were driving
through a remote part of the Wallowas in the late afternoon, and Nancy
said, 'Oh, look!' Four elk were crossing a wide creek and vanishing
through the snowdrift into the tree line. It could have been 1825."

From a friend's letter. I know how that felt.
Here at Camp Creek, where stream flow covers
voices from my neighbors' tents and campfires,
I am any Easterner first seeing these forests,
Mount Hood, its pyramid of snow, the forest firs.
Shock turning to Joy, the I Ching coins I threw yesterday.
In the first place and the last place,
the progress to joy, the struggle through knife-edge mountains,
to wake up out of dark and damp
above some spiritual timberline,
what wind and water tell us,
snow and rock and elk,
what might remain in our hearts.
Drinking Syrah and reading Rumi
in the loneliness of a new century,
I think of some calicoed woman
leaving her life behind,
sewing machines and cedar chests,
her fragments in the wagon ruts,
not knowing that she will live on
the sweet turns of the Willamette,
planting as I did last year a yellow rose,
Harison's Yellow, my great-grandmother's rose,
which follows me from house to house
when so much else has been jettisoned.

I drink to traveling mercies, the ruts left
in the prairie grass and the elk that still
walk across the creek and vanish in the trees.

For an 8 a.m. Class in Sentence Fundamentals

The comfort of nouns, for example.
The touch of this cup, table, chair, child, friend.
Morning light's generous hand
opening outside the wide window,
the opening of the mind to its contents,
loyalty, truth, even evil,
spilling onto the page.

As hands touch one another,
the nouns reach out for prepositions,
conjunctions, these lists that I offer
that bridge the shape-shifting
of nouns or the motion of verbs,
a motion that proves
we are always alive,
even in our states of being.

Adjectives scissor the edges of everything,
the qualities of the single white cup I hold.
Adverbs answer our questions,
tell us how
these rules and anomalies
will become flexibilities,
where to sit waiting
when the door suddenly
opens to sentences,
to what extent we are connected in sentences:
I am just like you.
You are my good friends.
We will work hard.
We are always together.
So many careful students
of this busy world.

My 8 a.m. Class Admits to Tears
After reading A Lesson Before Dying

I'm grading midterm question 8
about crisis and resolution from
the ex-Southerner who works at Bi-Mart,
when he tells me he "wipes away a tear."

Earlier this month my favorite tribal member
told the class she never reads books
but cried into cold bathwater over this one.
My row of athlete women argued
about how long, where, and when they cried,
while three just barely men in the back
hunched their shoulders like lost birds
caught in the coastal storm outside.

Halloween rain, a hard-time town,
the news hunting us, terror-stricken,
through the thickets of our lives,
while in the book's last chapter
several major characters fall down kneeling
as a poor man walks to electrocution.
Shocked too, this Monday we stumbled
from class, bowing over paperbacks
rain- and tear-stained,
and tonight I'm grading tests
with too many A's to suit
the administration.

I admit to believing, word after prayer,
(I got it wrong in Sunday school,
I've got it right now), that the right tears
will set anyone free.

Corrida

Guadalupe Boys Home, 1976

We watch from the office, how gently
your father puts your suitcase
in the bright-white pickup
where he mostly carries gardens.
You are his oldest son, your name tells us
you are from a royal house,
Victor Villareal.
Your father will not speak to us.

After you cut school for six weeks,
you had to learn your lesson,
were placed for six months sixty miles from home.
Once a week with the social worker,
twice a week with the counselor,
daily reading with the Anglo blond,
your Homeboy sign "La Stephanie" above her desk
that you lean on when you talk of La Rita,
your cheekbone tattooed with a tear,
rain on a cliff face.

Here only old Anglos wear khakis.
No one can cut your strong black hair.
At their fair, dizzy from the Tilt-A-Whirl,
you stumble down the midway
against blond boys and girls
who look away and carnies
who compare tattoos.

Everyone here except the cook
speaks T.J., old folks Spanish.
You begin to forget what to say
to Mouse and the other Homeboys.
Every day you sit in the kitchen,
every night in the dorm you
smoke weed in the dark,
lie naming the streets,
Homeboy turf, Spring Street,
Sixth Street, Clay.

While you sleep,
boundaries change.
Rita fucks Mouse.
The yellow walls on Clay
are tattooed, "Bloods Rule,
Homeboys Die."

In school you become
un milagro, a miracle, a mask,
who fills out applications,
studies our maps,
wins the ride home in
the shining pickup,
Victor Villareal.

Spring Street, Sixth Street, Clay.
Delores, sister of Rita,
waits at the park.
Your strutting khakis
have a crease so sharp
they cut the welcome-home cake.
The snake's head shotgun rises
above the smoked window
of a blue '60 Chevy—
you fall.

Blue Linoleum

I'm sorry. I can't tell you who she is.
I heard the words *blue linoleum*,
and I was there, eyes sore like hers
from pine oil suds in the galvanized bucket,
on her knees on blue linoleum,
the litany of bend and push, dip and wring.
A back kitchen at dusk, the streetlight comes on,
shines on a sea of blue where her hands
are deliberate creatures, starfish finding their way.

Her hands are red flags thrown down,
just finishing the bad place by the back door
when he leaves the sagging couch,
marks the shining squares, and goes.
The blond daughter watches from the edges,
escapes for cigarettes, wonders how
women can ever rise from blue linoleum, go
to a bed, and gasp for love.

The house is an empty cave. The streetlight
comes on and shines on blue linoleum.
Can you find the gray house,
the silent house, from what I say?
I do not know her name, oh angels,
there on her knees, so clean,
so alone—oh rescuing angels,
speak to her.

Amazons

She taught them to ride
on a cow-hocked gelding,
the young girls,
to straddle with curveless legs,
soft, hairless cleft,
the fat castrati's spine,
all swallowing corral dust
like an acrid wish unspent.

The young girls.
A temple frieze
against the dust motes in the barn,
arms delicate and slow and dreaming
as the curry comb sends currents flickering
down a muscled flank.
Light hands.

They learn light hands.
Gentle, perpetual control,
bound to the steel restraint
between the gelding's jaws.
"Feel, the horse is frightened now,
and you must still your fears in quelling his.
He sees dark rivers
where rain fell by the barn."

And in dry twilight,
the gelding and the woman
ride to rangelands,
talk like immigrants of deserts,
dream of journeys herding mares
to green-rimmed water wells,
converse through quivers down his belly
that pass electric to her womb.

Light hands.
She learns the discipline of easy arms,
her fingers stroke the hollow place
along her lover's spine
to send him shuddering to rest.

For Donald

You hit *Escape* out of our system sooner
than I expected, old programmer, old smoker,
gasping air from silver cylinders last Christmas,
dying with Cheyne-Stokes inhalations, the death rattle,
just when your roses were blooming,
catching your breath at last.

Toward the end your thirty-years lover
carried you, the prednisone that freed
your lungs breaking bone after bone
in hairline cracks that branched and spread.

Like the roots and trees you tended so long,
old gardener, like complicated directories,
roots and trees lost in the computer's memory.
Gardening just memory to you,
all you could share was advice,
this rose, that season.

But at the flickering screen,
your acolyte and something more,
creating and changing data and systems
there at the keyboard, our fingers
danced with each other breathlessly.

Your lover has given me
the computer's table, a metal skeleton.
In the photograph he sent, you are seated
before the screen, and the computer's body
is safely held there.

Where I will install my own system,
and among the branching subdirectories
create a path to those eccentric programs
you could never make me understand
and I can't remember

if you said plant daphne or peony
for the strong perfume, but in our gardens,
I will keep breathing for you
as long and as deep as I can.

Travelers

1.
This summer she learns words for the next journey.
Lists float, prayer flags, handkerchiefs waving goodbye,
her own language a street vendor's shout,
disappearing behind her.

With the lists pasted on refrigerator and cupboard,
she sees herself telling the new country she is *profesora*, *esposa*.
Words murmur as she drives, *allí, aquí, autobús*. Guides.
Children wanting chocolate, photos, a pen
to write down her name.

She imagines hours at the airport,
hearing the words fly by her,
pigeons in the eaves.
She almost recognizes them
as they fly past, she is almost there
on pages of summer wings.

2.
He lines them up,
Spanish workman's knife
next to Italian switchblade
beside Tibetan farmer's scythe.
For conversation, pulls them out
on the job, in bars, tells each barter
over again, carves each memory
as the knives fill up the tray by his chair.
Bright streets. Sleeping countries.

Or opens and shuts the blades in lamplight,
hearing railways and bazaars with each click,
the reassuring sounds of foreign tongues.

Teotitlán del Valle

For such a long time, the bus tries to escape the city.
The conductor, who will be sixteen someday soon,
slaps the side of the bus like a conga,
and all the world huddles in the aisle.
The woman beside me has red ribbons
braided in black hair.

Once in Ladakh a small woman
with brown yarn in black braids
sat on my lap, the Dalai Lama's smile
swinging in her locket. The whole bus sang.
If we sit close enough on these journeys,
such a song, even with clicks and half tones
and places in my mouth where my tongue gets lost,
such a song blossoms, hibiscus floating,
the bus drifting down the windy road.

Just breathe.
Someone will always help you
catch your bus, find the right stop.
There corn rises from the milpas.
A burro has grown a hump of sticks and leaves,
small hooves that dance a quick time.
These are short lives and slow gestures.
Every song from the driver's radio
has enough words about the heart, the soul.
"*Buen provecho*," I always say
to anyone still seated
when I leave the *comedor*.
"Yes," they say, they smile.
"*Que te vaya bien*."

Soon the bus finds the city again.
We peel off from each other, garlic cloves.
Today I was not lost in the market.
Tomorrow, I say, I'll begin again,
buy words from another town.

Descent

As the plane comes closer to Guatemala,
a tropical storm thunder and lightning,
the woman behind me pulls out her rosary,
the businessman beside me gives me his card.

I'm not much safer though.
The plane rises and falls.
It has forgotten how to fly,
is just a boat on a treacherous ocean.

I look down.

Words from a childhood book rush toward me:
Volcano—the rosary shines with its sparks.
Lava—the cone is exploding.

And I, northern I,
am so close to parrots
that call my panic,
a boa's twist and fall,
hot sheen of coffee,
the smell of sex in the orchids.

Fold after green fold
I swoop and drop
plumed, a quetzal.

I am a jungle.
I never knew that before.

Oaxaca Journal

Sometimes it's enough just to live,
let the day slip past, buttery,
melon cut in small slices,
the wet morning song of the parrot
among rain-shadowed leaves.
Page after page turns, words fill us,
whisper and wander past—
how patient the streets twist through the heart,
through the wide darkness available,
for rent, for sale, for love.

Bougainvillea blossoms like insect wings
fly into the water glass, cross our footsteps.
Have you brought the darkest chilies,
the reddest tomatoes, the strongest yoke
home from market? Then that's why
your bare feet widen in the dust,
why in the Tlacolula churchyard
yours is a small circle of "oh,"
a mango, papaya, smile.

The day ends again in rain.
The mango-flesh sky falls open, darkens.
How quiet we become, the rooms of ourselves,
lace over the windows piercing the last light.
Gladiolas are quenched candles,
market tarpaulins soft hands that capture
the barters and successes that we awoke to.

Take down the sky.
Twist the clouds to ropes.
In afternoon rain, children
become old women, then turn to trees
in this country with bells at every hour,
flowers and candles on the graves.

Amina from Kashmir

Your father is spending all his money on this.
There will be musicians. He especially wants drums.
Every day the tailor paddles to your houseboat,
fills your trunk with a lifetime of clothing.
You cry a little when he leaves, chopping vegetables
while your younger brother and his tutor chant Koran,
humming like the sewing machine, while your mother
squats beside you, scrubbing pots and telling you to behave.
Your younger sister on the rooftop giggles with the tourists.

You want quiet. And you don't.
The school picture your best friend found of him
hides in your slipper, as if a soft beard beginning
and a mole by his nose could be enough information.
You count the world in twos, the tourists holding hands,
your mother's wide hips in bed by your father's skinny backside,
the silence of possibility, boats on the lake that come and go,
your boat floating toward something unspoken and unseen.

Yugoslavia

I have lost Yugoslavia.
Someone who said *"Dobar Dan"* to me
is no longer alive, no longer walks with a donkey,
no longer stands in a wide field watching sheep.
My five white cups from bombed-out Karlovac are lonely—
perhaps I will never count to more than five again.
My stomach is lonely for *burek* and thin red wine.
My eyes are lonely for autumn,
red peppers hanging from every rooftop,
orange corn heaped in every yard,
the white spine of limestone *karst*
throughout what I thought was one country,
where someone no longer walks.

O *svetis*, saints dancing on church walls—your silence,
while pencil points of minarets write screams.
I wrote a list of wishes for the auto mechanic in Sarajevo,
the words, the Berlitz told me, were one country's language.
What did I really say to you?
What would I say now?

I have five white cups and saucers that sit on a shelf together.
I want a country of the human heart that will not shatter
into neighbor bombing neighbor,
the old robberies of religion begun again.
In dreams I cross the vanished Mostar bridge,
searching for all the mouths that once shaped greetings
in a country that I have lost.

Woman at the Window

Guanajuato, Mexico, 1992

I no longer dream. Old women give up those times
of prophecy, those noisy children jumbling
past on present, the nights reversing reason.
Once the stairway beyond my bedroom shook
with the past jostling itself awake
to intrude, present and past shrieking
like barkers at a fair, like butchers and bakers,
the tinwork tapping my shoulder in the market,
vendors thrusting desires I refused into my bag
while I hurry along, desperate for morning.
Now in the bed where I have always been alone,
I am a sailor shrouded in canvas tossed
nightly over the gunnels, loving
the sea's embrace of forgetfulness.

I drink tea in Papa's chipped cup,
place my lips over his. I wear mourning,
clothes of spongy black shadows, though their texture
no longer evokes voices. After my dreamless nights
I linger dressing, give the girdle and camisole time
to do their straight black work. The artist Rivera
was here born in Guanajuato, although I claim
no acquaintance, another five-storied house
only five winding streets away. I have not
seen it for forty years. Only the market
and the cathedral draw me daily from the house.
Then I return my beads to the bedpost, anchor
the straight-backed chair to the window,
hypnotize myself with the first sun.

Corner by corner the crowded blocks of house
fold into intricate shapes, warmth and absence of warmth.
Sleep dissipates beneath my gaze, a milky gauze rises,
a curtain softens the shadowed houses until noon
when all differences between walls disappear.
Obsession with light and shadow is my day.
Mornings when the houses chant most strongly
their stained-glass mass of rose and blue, lime and gold,
I stare at no one and everyone, a mask
looking back at masks, watching sun and shadow
split apart. Someday I will burn these backless slippers
and walk away, each day I expect a trumpeter,
some veteran of a pageant past to break
this tyranny of silence, call me forth.

Instead Ortega the lawyer appears at nine
like a wooden train crossing our shared plaza
carrying rolls and milk in a plastic sack,
first motion to break the patterned light and shade.
My crumpled hands at their white crochet look like that sack.
Next his son like some lesser streetcar stumbles past
in his schoolboy shorts, his schoolboy naked knees,
a milky smile given to someone who leans from another window.
The moon is still a sugared circle, a roll he bites.
Someday he might smile at me. Someday someone
should turn cartwheels or dance across these cobbles
where schoolchildren are arrayed in line after line
like buttons or beads being strung to silence.

From this window I have looked so closely at life,
it has been a criminal whose face
I have studied each day,

unable to give the changing mask a name.
The lottery tickets old Aurelio hangs
in the grocery tempt me. Buying a long strip
I could tear off one by one and my hands
might win, take instruction how to grab
life's mysterious messenger sleeve, how
to move among the butterfly students
in the plaza so that their wings brush
gold onto my black clothing, no longer
the soundless wind that divides their flocks,
passing untouched among their beauty.

Last night there were fireworks. No one knew
the reason. Not the Assumption or Saint John's Day.
All year I wait for my saint day, for Easter,
for the condescension of His birth. Each day
I wait for the lit candle, the resumption of dawn.
I fear the day might jump its track without me,
Ortega and his boy might not appear,
the moon not be eaten by sunlight,
the cliff edges of houses might crumble
and vanish to a speechless rubble, my life
a silent gesture from arthritic hands
that do not even hold each other well.
I speak and no one finishes my sentences.
Dreamless, no one dreams of me.

Although I no longer dream, I still wake anxious,
needing to set the wrongs of the house to rights.
I wash my underclothes, hang their shriveled
breasts and thighs secretly in the patio,
let my sheets with their dry-leaf smell vanish

with the maid Felicia, welcome them back
clean-faced as children, a miracle.
What rooms are filled by this body,
whose body wears these fabrics?
At forty I looked down while I dressed
against the church's injunction. My calves
had narrowed, my skin no longer leapt and danced,
my belly swelled, my breasts drooped like any woman's.
There was no dispensation for dry celibacy.

I live in three rooms, the black-and-white scarcity
of the kitchen, accumulated histories of the bedroom,
shining parental walnut of the parlor that turns to dust
then reappears in the constant worship of my cloth.
I mix my polish of brandy, lemon, and oil that clings
to my fingers like the priest's soft hand, the Magdalene's hair
that washed the Savior's dusty toes. In the bedroom,
two lovers once slept embraced, whispered what they dreamed
here where I cross myself before the Guadalupe,
bend across starched pillows flat as my breasts,
dust the dead pair in the wedding photograph,
wondering if one parent dreamed, one did not.

Last week a photographer looked back at me.
He moved in the plaza with a hypnosis I recognized,
his Cyclops eye searching the yellow wall, the shadows
of flower pot, electric wire, the cornice
where a young dove flutters to the edge, retreats.
What did he see in my window? My body halved,
black arms and torso drooping from the rectangle.
What language interprets me and my world within?
As the wave and the undertow are partners,

in the act of seeing we joined, morning and evening,
blank pages filled by the eye's dictation.
Another celebrant of black and brilliance,
he traveled toward me from a long distance,
met at the table of the day where we feast.

I have not seen that traveler since then.
In some other country, does he resurrect my vigil?
My cloth makes a perfect circle, a sun centered
in a whirlpool, then follows my fingers on the window
as a priest follows the shining cross up the aisle.
The morning air stands beside me like a sister,
like a young tree with butterflies ready for migration.
I will drink from Mama's china cup, send Ortega's child
for thin biscuits that cross my tongue with an angel's kiss,
find the breath that lifts the dove on the roof to flight,
the butterfly students to dance together, the trumpet
to mark redemption I earn for faithful vision. The world
is born through vision; the heart travels through the eye.
There is no celebrant unworthy of communion with the day.

Inspired by a 1993 monotype by Galen Garwood, Port Townsend, Washington, and by Guanajuato itself.

III
Family Tree

Arithmetic

My father's mother adds to the world
two lives. With the second birth,
she is subtracted.
In those days,
when a farm wife lay
in the dark silence of hemorrhage,
the bed was tilted
against blood's gravity
until the doctor came.
She slid to her grave nonetheless.

My other grandmother adds five,
minus the first son, gone in fever.
My mother remembers
splashing puddles in the rain
to make the baby laugh,
her memory all that's left of him
before he buried my grandfather's smiles
away with his.

The next generation
multiplied by twos and fours,
all surviving, fourteen cousins,
rubbed close as kernels
in the soft silk and tough husk of family,
spat out to breed,
some in twos, some in ones,
some of us none, equations incomplete.

My sum lay unfinished
in the doctor's bowl.
Now, carrying into the future
only some chancy growths,
tumors common to the childless,
faced with the subtractions of surgery,
I ponder the results
of that embrace of zero.

Letter to Alaska

Brother, because
we share our blood,
when you walk
stony river bottoms,
my feet hurt too.
I steady myself from slipping,
ease forward against currents
that flow past us in loving strokes,
your shadow as you go solitary
in that open land.

Because we share our blood,
its genes of isolation,
months pass without a letter's pulse
to beat between us.
My compass still points north.

So little sun this spring,
I've seldom seen a shadow.
Your letter came today.
Had you known
how weak the power
of the poles had grown,
how dangerous our lives are,
traveled without a shadow?

After the Visit

Nephew,
with the wind's spiral this feather
left on the dashboard
could fly north and find you.
Some seagull discard, shell gray,
camouflage scrap, its hollow tube
could float above the sand
that speckles seats and carpet
until this burgundy sedan
is ocean fragrant, has enough marine
to be our private island.

There, Crusoe and Friday, we could tell our stories,
syllables that the east wind takes.
I warn you we will change, a little wave,
more foam rising, tides closing in.
This the narrative I learn from you.
When you kiss goodnight,
bathed and gleaming
in dinosaur pajamas,
you smell, my seagull,
of distance, you are
my sailor waving goodbye
climbing the stairs, and I
am wishing bon voyage
for us both because
what else can we ever do,
riding above the riptides
and sneaker waves
of time.

Farm Women

The men mostly lived by the weather,
stood on the front porch for long spaces,
deciding if hay could be made,
enough cows could be pastured,
enough milk in bright cans
should rattle up Creamery Hill.

We women
had to have secret ways and means.
We carried them in apron pockets,
hid them among the handkerchiefs
the children gave for Christmas.
How to get by.
We stood for long mornings
at the kitchen sink
wondering.

Mary

You needed a husband, I decided.
And married the hired hand at forty,
no secrets about him, he'd
been part of the farm so long
like the black mule or a gray fencepost.
No babies, though.
After he died, one way
to go on was housekeeping
for old men, old women
until my eyes failed.
Then the outlines of

cupboards and chairs
could disappear to dust
and I could get by
on what sounds gave—
the snowy day in the radio static,
the plastic curtains here in the home
that flap like cowbirds rising from a stubbled field
as the plow cuts through.
The nurse's keys jingle like harness rings,
Jessie's daughters coming up the stairs
sound like windows opening after a storm,
their voices are lights coming on.
I've put my money away
for Jessie's girls.

Jessie

My sister-in-law had it right.
Live thrifty, right to the end.
Bind life together in a careful count—
robins return, written down in dime-store diary,
summer boarders migrate in and out,
even yet they come to see me here.
My daughters complain about the busy street,
the nursing home smell. They don't know
what I keep track of here, how the nurses say,
"You have more visitors than anyone."
Write your name down for me, everyone does.
Like Mary, I can no longer see
the careful schoolmarm script I learned.
After the first boy died, 1919,
after Joe died at sixty,

I learned to hold on to what would best
fill those secret empty spaces—
which grandchild are you?

Thelma

It's no secret.
You get by with hard work.
My grandchildren learned that.
My boy married Jessie's middle girl,
my grandchildren are hers too,
and then she shared the rest of hers—
they call me "aunt."
I hid words of love away, cooked them away—
I have secrets hidden in the recipes I left behind.
Stitched the words down, quilt after quilt.
You have to keep track.
Cups of flour. The smallest stitches.
Listen in on the extension
to words of love
the children give away.
In the last hour,
when I asked the minister to find
final words for me, I saw rows
and rows of daily bread shining,
knew I left no debts nor debtors,
and my hands rose
like white handkerchiefs
rested in the hands
of the children
I loved.

Fever—1924

She puts ice on my tongue that tastes of spring water,
the wet handkerchief held to my forehead is a snowball.
I should call her Mrs. Hunt, but I call her Jessie,
she was here when the room was blazing bright,
now she blankets me in darkness.

I asked for the Cinderella story, I think.
She has been reading it for days, her voice steady
when I begin to float, when I say to myself,
"I am Elsie, I am twelve, that is Jessie's voice,"
a rope in the greedy waves, the room's dark shapes.

I hear voices sometimes through the walls,
so many women, are they quilting, they can't be canning
in my mother's bedroom, my sick brother quiet now,
his crying hurt my head.

Someone sobs like Ma did when hail hit the whole harvest.
Jessie opens the door, my aunt carries a white bundle like laundry,
Jessie says, "My boy too, five years ago this month,"
stares at my blanket-covered window a long time.

Then reads Cinderella again, her voice promises
spring water, dry sheets when the fever breaks,
a prince's arms to find me, bring me back
from the shadowed edge where I spin and turn.
Jessie's voice.

Based on a letter by Elsie Westbrook after my grandmother Jessie's death.

Two Across

The grandmother afternoons:
the old woman sleepy beside me,
our crossword done, leftover words we murmured,
"When?" "remember," "cousin," "home,"
the cluck of hens in the barn,
our green porch rockers matching rhythm,
the fan shushing from upstairs.

She read from her diaries, not golden letters,
but ordinary as her slipped cotton stockings,
sturdy syllables of black mail-order shoes,
recipes in the margins, the first date the robins sang.
Below us the lake held a rowboat, one oar left drifting,
a fish rose to a mayfly and fell back to ripples,
lily pads grew thick as clotted cream.
We had one summer just like that,
interlocked and numbered with ordinary words.

In Her Kitchen

For Phoebe Shotwell

I sit down again in this calm kitchen of the heart,
swallow the fragrant hours, fresh bread split open
while we lean toward each other
over strong coffee and a book,
while we unfold our fabric,
sister's daughter, heart's mother,
fill the seated times between
first meal and second,
last meal and the moment
when we leave the room.
I turn off the light, look back—
we remain, our faces
transparent as cooking odors,
whispers of what we fed each other.
The pause before the lights go out.
The hungry doors of time.

My Aunt Speaks

She counts her eggs in epic couplets,
names new calves in villanelles,
praises the daughter who marries a farmer
in sonnet scheme.
In iambs and dactyls
through the dusty lanes,
calls home the cows
rhymes all her days
with lovely chores
my aunt stores
in her speaking.

Postcard: Family Reunion 1905, Nebraska
My grandfather visits his brother and sisters.

Eight of us moved west.
Weighted by eastern habits,
first stumbled under hard prairie light,
drowned our vision in endless rivers,
burrowed mole blind in tornado cellars,
were blizzard buried by long white winters.
We nearly disappeared from this photograph.
Our starched shirts and dresses speak
familiar language, but we're translated now,
dreaming in homestead words.
Drought, wind, horizon.

Welcome, younger brother, who fed
mother, father from yourself until their deaths,
who stands among us now.
Will you leave the folded Jersey hills
where you've been caved, come blinking
to what we at last have learned to see?
Join the potluck, pose beside us,
let the shutter's click become
your territory, homestead too.
Learn to love our world's edges,
where the sandhill cranes go traveling,
syllables of wind across our hard-won land.

Gospel According to Phoebe

Today my niece in Oregon calls for news.
My husband is doing fine after his fall,
bandages and stitches gone.
He rides the new elevator up the stairs just fine.
I'd rather walk up. And argue with my daughters.
Sleeping on the couch while he slept in his chair
wasn't bad. We never got a bed in, the way the kids wanted.
I don't sleep that good anymore anyway.
The niece is like me, like all the Hunt girls.
We read in the night, and the men in our beds
sleep to the sound of pages turning.
Seventy years he has complained
and gone back to snoring,
gotten up to milk cows just fine.
Last year when I was so sick, though,
all night he sat up by the bed,
watching me breathe. Tonight
I'll get the daughter up the road
to take us to another niece's farmhouse.
I expect there will be a nice crowd,
maybe forty people. Our family.
Hay prices are up. The weather is dry and cold.
There, I have given my niece the good news.

Riding Lesson
For Kate

With this year's braces glinting,
you wave across the arena
on a bay mare who turns because
you have put your leg against her
just as the instructor says.

We tense at thunder,
one horse jumps, not you or yours,
you giggle as the bay mare backs,
your fingers knuckled on the reins.
My fingers curl.

And though you never slid to life
between my legs, my small blond foal,
my cousin, you still turn to me
when you figure-eight, smile
from the cradle of the lope,
count with me the heartbeat trot,
straight and sure.

I worry, are you tired?
Yes, later in the dentist's waiting room
you lean against me, nearly boneless,
tangle your blond mane and mine
until we smell of school and sweat,
strange orange candy and the chocolate taste
of saddle soap and dust and horse.

When you were barely there, the incubator baby,
the blue dress I bought for you a doll's size,
we all rode horses for you in our dreams.
And now this horse beneath you moving forward,
my legs can feel that too.

Surface and Strata

Stepson,
you call from LA after your birthday,
a candle flame wish in your voice,
ask if change takes place under the surface,
if each of these slow summer days can be marking you.

No, not like your tattoo did.
More like night on the Mojave,
communions barely heard that leave
secret languages tracked across the sand,
so many stars the skin is scraped raw enough
to answer every breath of air.
In daylight, just lunar surface,
plants that never seem to grow.

Would it make sense to describe that earthquake city
where you live, where I lived?
How I woke one morning,
saw the corners of my room split apart,
stood in the doorway, watched the street
a beast shaking off its skin,
its ocean self revealed,
deep uneasiness in the troughs.

After the earthquake, strata came to a new relation,
something was stirred up, but the land settled again.
We hardly noticed the aftershocks,
the palm trees trembling on the night horizon.
Beneath us, the earth kept moving.

Still, I can see how this summer seems
the slow ambulations of not much going on.
Drunks curse outside your window, a block from the all-night movies
where twenty years ago I brushed against them restless in the darkness.
Your new address—my footsteps must still echo in the flat upstairs.

When we speak like this, stepson, stepmother,
two travelers assigned adjoining seats,
we struggle with family languages,
to rise above the weighted air of myths.
That week we bargained for your first car
among the deceptions of the lots,
we wrote a short novel of ourselves.
In the subtext we decided
to make the words between us
hold their value.
We hardly knew we'd changed.

First Cousins

Only because your daughter insists
I see her first prom dress,
its tulle wings, the black lace
where her fledgling bones show through,
am I here, talking credit cards with your wife,
showing your son his face in an ancestor's photograph
while you wash winter dirt from the family cars outside.

Once we were apple-tree climbers, tricycle friends,
golden babies photographed rolling in pillow feathers.
One day on the Hoboken train,
the conductor asked, "Are you twins?"
Now, distant and domestic on opposing coasts,
I migrate here yearly and you
look past me, never speak my name.

Except today. My borrowed car hums in the driveway,
but you want to tell me how one hundred snow geese
landed in your field, how widgeons flood the thawing ponds.
Your joined hands show the Vs of geese.
Wild turkeys are everywhere these years, we agree,
and yes, we both know last week's story,
a single sandhill crane flying from field to field
across two counties, followed by birders,
and we ask each other, "Why just one?
Do cranes mate for life?" but we don't know.
What language are we speaking
while drifts of feathers fill our hands?

IV
Stopping Time

Stopping Time

The day pools down, a lake of air.
I tilt the contents of a sorted desk
into the burn barrel, snowy fragments.

Watching my signature twist
on a thousand old checks,
I smell memories rising,

but allow each barter of the past
to turn ash gray unconsidered,
no more to do with me than today's junk mail.

I halt the moving hour, stopping
even spring grass growing beneath me
as I stand balanced,

a field worker with my basket,
holding earth separate from sky,
then walk away.

The screen door slams.
The swallows on the horizon lift,
the final cloud escapes.

The scraps that float
above the barrel glow.

Balancing, Bowing

She is always thinking about love,
who to, how much to,
should she have, why didn't she,
is this, was this, could this be, the right love?
The mountain of questions keeps her sleepless—
but it is "in breath, out breath,"
it is the command form "love now,"
she distracts herself from.

Let her be an old cat and its windowsill both,
not even thinking "grateful," just noting "life, warm, now."
Let her be her visiting nephew, who on tiptoe
turns on morning lights, then, "done, Auntie,"
trusts the next task without knowing
today his plane will leave.
Each day let her try Tree Pose, Dancer,
let her steadiness surprise her, let her heart
live in Child's Pose, easiest of all.

Storage System

I've begun to date my life
with strange years—1987, 1964.
Tuesday in the supermarket
1953 scuttled out of my pen,
crabbed its way onto the check,
written as if an age-spotted hand covered mine.

Blind muscles search hallways for the past,
my sixteen-year-old fingers
etching dates on school papers,
next shaping my lips
to the waxy white of gardenias.
I lean in the mirror to another spring,
one I'd rather forget
that speaks through my hand,
coming back to talk it all over again.
The body knows no release,
hoards every slap, kiss, sleep, scald, ache.

Tonight, lightning bugs tangle around me,
and I am somehow five years old again.
The body keeps each impermanence.
My hands beneath the porch light
are transparent, luminous.
Torches. Guides.

Nocturne

Now light turns the corner,
strolls out of the neighborhood
like the last dog walker headed for a house
I can only wonder about.
Evening truths—this body cannot
forget its age, its hip and hand ache.
Also true—a constant girl lives
in this basket of flesh and bone,
no older than when she watched
night lightning off the Canyon's North Rim,
one summer when love was all catch and release,
the sweet tumble of bodies back to the stream.
She sorted the auguries, reached
across the deep to light's ripple.
Was there somewhere else besides here
she'd hoped to go? Never mind.
She still rises in my body, a silver fish,
and fisher and fish, we are one
in hopefulness.

Beauty

Once I wrapped my naked body
in an old blue curtain like a Grecian gown
and I was beautiful, I knew it,
dancing in a narrow room under the maples,
to a pop song, Saturday morning radio,
Perry Como, someone smooth, refined
as the satin gown I'd pledged
against my narrow hips, my breasts
just rising in soft bruises.
I was eleven, still tripping over dolls.
We still lived on the farm, the great silence
that comes from fields, from snow on the way,
my parents downstairs in the rooms
they kept closed against each other.
When I did what women don't admit to each other,
my fingers private between my thighs,
I danced a hoochie coochie, brought myself
future, wish, that a woman's life could be
this shining fabric, my body's sheen beneath.

Luck at the El Gato

I remember desire now,
that summer when the sun sprawled
Greek and immense in my shadeless room,
how I slept each afternoon,
dreamed while the sheets coiled
around my legs, sweating
until the bed stank,
a bruised hillside,
sage, thyme, coarse grasses.

Evenings I went dancing.
The jukebox played "*Volver, volver,*"
my chain of quarters never broke,
the tanned men passed the liars cup from hand to hand,
and dice like hidden soldiers rattled out.
One bad throw never counted much.
Some nights we drank until the next hot dawn.

The Lump

This beach stone fills my hand
like a breast fallen from a statue,
rubble on Greek steps
leading to the sea.
There is the moment monthly
when I test
whether a sculptor has turned me
similarly to stone.
Medusa glanced once, after all.
Then under the operating room's light,
its Aegean sun, I was
bedrock excavated and rescued.
The surgeon's jokes,
the nurse's hand in mine.
We are counting the minutes
until the anesthesia runs out,
cutting in and out of pain.
He gets it all, he says.
This stone in my hand.

One Season Goes

Watch the signs—milkweed blows
through fields of autumn sun,
shriveled birch leaves peel away,
petals of the turned year burn brown.
The seasons fall from my hands
shining chips left on the trails I blazed,
moonlit crumbs night birds steal from me.

It's all a canoe trip in Lewis and Clark territory,
a portage over rocks where we lose our balance.
We add up the beads of years, barter along
the boundaries of seasons, leave behind
tight skin, my young and easy braids,
carry our ragged lives, our voices
fading behind us in the forest.

One by one the seasons fall,
rope loops to hold our pilgrim hands,
dropping down the cliff face
toward our rest.

The First Year Married

Our new neighbor hates corners,
builds a round house,
with beets and tomatoes,
puddles of pumpkins,
fills a circle garden.

I welcome corners,
let the lines of this new house
flow from me,
books ranked rectangles,
cupboard doors shut clean.
I put my hands daily to some large design,
let garden rows run parallel,
journey and return by the same road,
iron sheets and my sky clean, smooth.

But your socks fill the corners,
books scatter from you in tornadoes,
you walk in the room
and I no longer balance
on my straight line.
Lately I fill jars
with full-blown roses.
They remind me
of clasped hands
fingers circling each other,
petals falling down.

The Quarrel

He washes, she dries, the salt and pepper shakers of marriage.
His hands, white-knuckled, afraid something glassy, intricate,
 will fly apart,
her face the winter surface of the window before her.
Whatever words littered the dinner table could be hung up
 like cups,
like steady stars light-years distant, already dying.
His shoulder blades, she sees,
jut like pot shards from the valley of his back,
her fingers have read familiar inscriptions other nights.
"We aren't like this, are we?" he says, breaking silence.
"We aren't like this," she wants to agree,
 putting the kitchen to rights.

Dream Sonnet

Nothing moves more quietly here than the cat,
dust floating toward her cream each morning
just before the clock chimes its warning.
Nothing more necessary than that—
stillness, a lamplight's pool. Darkness
covers yesterday's voices, each slipup
that coffee fragrance soothes, the cup's
warm weight I hold, the daily burden less.

Because last night I dreamed of you.
The Seine was fogbound. We had some errand.
Your hand warm when it slipped away. Deafened
by mist and marriage, I lost you. Nothing new.
I woke to silence. I cannot make the coffee sweet
enough to steady my heart's erratic beat.

This Year

The body becomes taciturn,
laconic its gesture, arousal the last thought
of a long day, easy to dismiss.

Go on, you transparent autumn days,
swifter than I to blaze and shadow,
to stretch thin the mauves of the damask rose.

Go on. I am still the playground's
youngest child, running to catch up.
I'll find accommodation.

If the flesh is always home,
then blind, I memorize again
its furnishings.

What I believe I lust for, lip color,
the pink knit dress, a man's body to cover mine,
has another name. All our lives we letter these names.

Then the prayers tied to the apple tree dissolve,
the parents die. No one calls the name
of the round unfocused baby,

given up, like a missed heartbeat,
friendships too—no one remembers the childish script,
the nicknamed note passed down the row.

So I turn to you in the night.
Maybe I dream you into other shapes I want to wear.
Perhaps I am still distant.

Or I may be the voice
who answers you from the garden

while you stack firewood in the shed,
two old lags still learning escape routes,
who in the night write with soft traceries
familiar hands across each other's flesh.

This Poem

Behind this poem is the man of the house
on his ladder, nailing boards against
how winter wants to turn the hands

writing this poem more arthritic.
Beyond this poem, my father's ashes huddle together
under hoarfrost, a few feet from his father's, his mother's bones.
Beyond this poem, you know the rest,
my mother lives, my brother, friends,
are owned by the poem. No escape now.

Around and across this poem, cheap lined paper,
the blue pen slips. The dog sleeps.
The owl's question, the wild turkeys waking
on their hemlock branch are walls around this poem,
castle of dreams and daylight, where
craving and letting go occurs,
inevitable grief, all in this poem,
container of what the world contains.

Within this poem, whatever space
the man of the house creates for the woman,
whatever she takes and will take,
comes and goes—the glance
the sun will later make,
the steady dissolve of frost,
grass emergent, syllable
and space between.

Report from the Bee Tree

Where did you find it?
Where the gravel road stays dark all day,
shaded by the oldest maple.
That's the bee tree.

When did you find it?
Last year. Then I forgot.
How the summer bees chant,
surround the air,
gold chains looped,
leaving the bee tree.

What do you see?
At 6 a.m. today
just a dead mass in cold air.
Only the knife-edge shine
of a single wing.
A great socket in the face of the tree,
the bees its watching eye.

Who else knows this?
Neighbor Geraldine.
But her husband, Louie the bee man,
died this spring.
The Valium she takes
makes her forgetful.
Some days I'm the only human memory
of the tree.

If you forget?

Histories pass.
Knowledge of great activities
is easily lost.
Why not of bees?

And if the bees forget?
They won't. They dance,
leave each day, return
on the leading strings of language,
their dance.

If they leave and don't return?
In Spain, I watched a village call back their bees
using stone on stone, a guttural knocking,
circling the church where the bees had swarmed.
A madwoman sang to them back at the hives.

Could you call them back?
Give stone its mate,
know the madwoman's song?
Dance like bees, weave
a light language of fragments?
Tell me again what you see.

Memory massed, history honeycombed,
knowledge dancing.

What will you do with your life?
I don't know. Day after day
I return to the bee tree.

V
Rink Creek Journal

Our First Words Each Day

We explain the sky again and again,
like Constable repeating cloud studies,
his brush writing down small bruises in the cumulus,
the long whistle of cirrus above the watermill.
The hour turns out like a pillowcase,
lavender and soap and dreams gone flat,
and I can't remember if I told you,
so I go on telling you,
one child whose words
mist to another through the window
as the school bus pulls away.
I say, "Blue as a gun barrel or the trout's side,"
you say, "No, a dusty plum."
Constable meantime goes on,
content with private language,
investigating the brush's angle,
the weight of cadmium and China white.
It is early. We still hold
the shells of our bodies close.
Silent, we could hear syllables of each other,
years of sky, summer, sea.
In Essex, for example, Constable
has memorized the cloudy day.

What Do I Know?

Only how darkness
grows less beyond
this narrow window,
how the sky fills
with a circle of swallows
who have belled the wind,
with their wingbeats
guiding its direction.

The fog nourishes the fir ridge,
the deer wakes and feeds
in its blackberry cave.
The kitchen clock ticks its minutes,
I hear the slow minuet of breath
easing out of my skin,
and I keep on with what I know,
watching from this couch
how words float to the page
like leaf shreds given over
to the creek flow.

Matins

      The morning waits, listens
for the daily wind to rise,
birds among dark leaves
the only ripple on the day's smooth surface.
Any word could become a bell,
first tinsel chiming, then swelling
to hold this clearing,
the fir ridge, the town beyond.
Any possibility could name itself and be born.
A foot could be set right,
a certain luck could occur,
a dark stranger could stand at the door waiting.
Luck all year.

      We could, the whole human family,
stand in relation to each other,
join hands under the canopy of the bell's sound.
And sometimes—our shells as hard
as the hazelnuts the squirrel pursues—
sometimes we open the fragrant meat of ourselves
to a lucky glance, the stuttering confidence.
A hand on another hand and the whole body is dignified,
stands healed and solid in the open air.
Luck. The grace of the stumble arrested,
of rising again under this quiet sky.
A bright door opens to the friendly room beyond.
A great bowl, sweet dough there on the counter,
waits to be shaped.

        The window
frames what I see,
the forest of possibilities.
I am grateful now,
calling my luck by its right name.
Upstairs, someone is sleeping.
Love. Hear how it sounds.

The Wheel

Today when the black dog and I
measure our morning mile,
she hears before I do
the kitten's shriek for rescue,
a cry like everything Siddhartha
learned about desire.

Kind belongs with kind, I believe—
return fledglings to the nest,
hunt for the litter perhaps hidden
in the nearby barn
where the great horned owl
drifts from the rafters
sniper silent,
blazes through fog
ardent for flight.

All beings in this place know now,
even as Siddhartha did at last,
the long power of death,
chill to the white void

opening under the feather's edge.
Life sleeps now in my coat pocket—
Siddhartha too learned
the cause of suffering and its antidote,
the sun that cuts the fog,
first heads, then tails,
the copper wheel.

In the Lane

The dog and I scatter the same
sparse gravel under our feet
each morning, startle

to the sudden rockets
of the same three frightened quail.
We push the fog, cold silk

on our faces, back to the ocean,
summon the creek to rise over riprap
again and again throughout the turning year.

In May, heat and rain,
the glow of salmonberry,
cool towers of foxglove from the shadows.

August. The Queen Anne's lace
shoots up again, dust catchers,
after the road crew's cutting.

October. The furred caterpillars
crossing the stones have never been so small.
A mild winter? A long hot autumn.

Small, repeated observations.
How white flowers cartwheel
like the Mayan calendar,

first yarrow, then Queen Anne's lace,
and pearly everlasting
ends the summer cycle.

How the dog forgets

and so knows best
how to rise and walk
the lane.

Obedience

This week the black dog
learns to come when called.
She hears my voice,
and from a far field
where she was happy hunting moles,
she comes, pink tongue like a river,
ears like breeze-caught kites
that almost come unfastened
in the slipstream as she answers.

Some days our lives
turn just on this,
love struck like a match
that blossoms ever ready.
We practice sit and stay.
The swallows rise
like sparks above the firs,
turn and return
across the open sky.

Abandoned

A friend says, "Yes,
I recall a house site there,
beyond the city reservoir
and your boundaries,
homesteaded in the '20s,
built close to the creek for water.
Such places are everywhere—
the family's name escapes me now."
The first clear day, I walk the land.
Crossing the creek, I lean breathless
against the apple tree that shelters
the rusted car, take a cutting
from the speckled climbing rose.

Maybe the blackberries remember
whether the rose fell
against the front porch or
over the garden fence,
whether the kitchen,
where someone propped her elbows
on a square wooden table,
drinking the creek and watching it tumble,
was large or small.
But in this hour
when the air slants like a looking glass,
a door stands open.
I take the cup she offers.
The creek still tastes the same.

The Green World

Before we bought this clear-cut land,
we did not understood
that impermanence
the Buddha spoke of.

Planting ourselves in the middle
of stumps and daisies,
building a house of mill seconds,
we work the ground slowly,
watch diesel cat tracks on the gyppo logged hillside
wash away, become alder thickets,
gather the blackberries that smother
abandoned cold decks and unburned slash heaps,
pick the foxglove, the yarrow, the pearly everlasting
covering the logger's footsteps.

The fir ridge awakens, grows taller.
We are dwarfed, withered
from lack of light around the cabin.
Some evenings, working in a garden
shaded more each year,
I study my hands, clubbed like paws
with garden dirt and leaf mold.
The green world comes closer,
breathes on my shoulder.
I may be a shadow,
mushroom dappled,
forest captured,
someday.

January

Too much rain.
The river rises,
closing the road to town.
The pump chokes on muddy creek water,
and the washer overflows.

It's all too difficult—
ice, losing balance,
snow and the silent telephone sulks.
Wind pushes a maple across the power line
as death one day will lay us down.

With just lamplight, I put aside written word.
Counting the pantry on my fingers,
I take the food allowed by weather,
wear a different skin,
unwashed, using less water,
live like so many in this suffering world.

With weather, as with meditation,
I begin with observation,
note the antiquity of chaos,
then step mindfully,
in mud, on ice,
breathe with the fir tree,
learn whatever gesture in the mind
that reaches through
an obscure time
to touch the face of order.

Hands

This spring the peppers refuse to grow,
the corn straggles along
like children headed for school.
The fish smell of fertilizer
coats my palms, my fingers ache
from weeding, from long hours
pretending to be rain,
ache from all this work I love.
Grow, I command. Prosper.
Then turn away, impatient hands
already busy with other chores.

Behind my back,
sun and rain drift in,
nights become warmer than blankets,
jalapeño blossoms come on like stars.
The corn swings eager arms to the wind,
echoes the heartbeat of sheets
rustling on the line.

This work of hands.
These empty spaces:
lines, rows, beds.
How weather, that ancient accident,
comes along, fills up the rows,
how at night, surprised
by a summer storm of the heart,
arms reach across the patient sheets
like green corn leaves,
kisses like blossoms,
like fiery stars.

K Country

That week when it seems everything disappears:
a favorite cat (raccoons go for the jugular, my old neighbor says),
a friend's children slide to death on the highway,
you and I talk on the telephone but cannot dissolve distance,
I cannot rescue my father from eighty
or his cousin's fields from flooding,
the cat's bones never appear among the ferns.

I will not match or memorize that pitch of silence.
Instead I tune to the country and western station,
and all across the state we strangers sing along,
shopping lists of words that know
we ache, we break,
crazy and blue we cross the lines,
and still return
by the river road in sunlight
where a cross and a wreath
wait by a missing rail,
moving on,
our eighteen-wheeler,
always hopeful hearts.

Flood Summer

The news magazine's map colors the family farm
safe from danger, but I step in and out
of high water all summer,
the lapping sound of impermanence,
the cool rise flooding the heart.
June. Gray bars of rain against
the drum of an empty house.
Your long absence deafens the landscape.
Raccoon or coyote takes the cat in July,
a scream ripples a night of beaten flat waters.
Even the rusted pickup left at the junkyard
is a loss, a twenty-years' familiar gone.

Then in August the last death
in a year of epitaphs. Black watermarks.
I whisper the losses, as at four
I dropped words after stones
into the cistern's dark tunnel,
the underground stream.
Donald, Rita, Maxine, Alfred, Bill—
the ordinary names we give to miracles
astound me.

The Month of Forest Fires

August breeds burning—
the hot gaze of summer lasts too long.
The dry land tangles fire and dust, dust and fire.
Each step ignites a plain
where breathlessness
goes on forever.

The young polish naked arms and legs
to be machines for embracing.
They cannot be still or be alone.
Even on the hottest days they rush
to burn one body against another.
The girl lets the screen door slam
behind her again and again,
no end to the times
she can turn her life to fire.

The woman sets sprinklers to salvage the corn,
follows their sighs through a chaste night,
thinks of the method of Demeter's grief,
her longing for the lovers' heat to be done.
The next months cannot come too soon
after this endless sunflare, Olympic crownfire.

The alteration of time in the tempo of desire.
Late one afternoon someone waits on the stairs,
then the tangle of arms and legs,
lip and tongue, the hour
holds its breath around them,
the footsteps leaving are hot ash.
And a memory.
She would have let that hour
burn again and again.

The creek goes dry,
the woman longs to find
a spring on the land, searches
for the seepage signal,
bees and rank grass
rising from the brown mat.
Who wouldn't surround
August with water,

fill this catch basin
of motionless air,
end the long drought
of yearning?

No one can die
like this
forever.

Black Bear

At first sight of you, I thought a man
had hiked our boundary path barefoot, a giant.
Your paw print gouged deep into spring mud
was like a frightened glance in a mirror.
I asked a shadow, "Where are you going now?"

Once someone saw you near the creek,
your snout questioning the summer air.
Then you ran away, drawn by shyness, a child's pull toy.
Guests who knew your language found scat
on the deer trails, bark rubbed by your back.
I wished then I had taken a cast of that footprint.
If Crusoe had not found Friday, wouldn't a token
of how the earth remembers have comforted him?
So I forgive if you, not coyote or raccoon,
killed last summer's cat.

Yesterday the new neighbor finds bones and shell casings.
Her cabin's last owner loved Christ and the shotgun.
I picture him at daily prayers, then rising to hunt.
Somewhere you scratched the earth a last time.
When we walk, the dogs circle spaces that seem empty to me,
snapped alder saplings, the creek's still shadows,
today quivering at a patch among the ferns.
But I don't kneel beside them.
In this absence I cannot greet you.
In this forest one less shadow
moves across the land.

Loss

Some days pass when
I don't think of loss at all.
Throughout the full moon
deer strip the apple branches
until the night's crevices ache
with persistent echoes, and lying awake,
I give them an entire yellow harvest,
saving only the red tree within the garden fence for myself.

What we give up gladly—
haven't we all gasped,
getting back like a bad address
the memory that labels us
fool, careless, angry, indiscreet.
I have forgotten the slap of a friend's hand.
I have forgotten old debts. I have.
In Rink Creek on hot summer days,
I walk back and forth on broad stones,
hear nothing over the roar.

Remember, the morning hours between one and four
are most dangerous for theft.
The bank vault of the blue night,
the shadowed empty pools of lawn
and the deer waiting for the dog to sleep.
All losses numbered by birthdays and cycles
arise and walk with the skinny grace of deer,
cry in circles around the house,
the copper strands woven by the owl call.

Those nights in endless lists I count
occasions when we balance to the penny's edge,
the step forward, the step backward permissions of life—
the transformation the doe finds
rising from its shining hooves
to teeter in the blue night under an apple tree,
chewing leaf after leaf,
her food also her balance point,
so that when she consumes what holds her,
she finds herself grounded again.
The deer knowing how it feels
to see the moon one day past its prime
through lattice branches
that seemed like food forever.

Discovery

Watching the slender bridge of a new day,
its nearly violet opening across the fir ridge,
I am as unsure as the factory cat
who yesterday found grass for the first time,
discovered how a tree's branches lead ladderlike upward.
I leave last night between the married sheets.
Nothing else here struggles with the future, its close-fitting sleeve.
When I was a child, spelunkers asked permission each summer
to search the cave beyond the pond,
took me along at seven and eight years old.
They were marking all entrances and exits,
recording formations like sharp words, puddled tears.
In one tunnel I couldn't breathe or stand,
too frightened to reach forward or shrink back.
Somewhere their maps fill up a book.
As those maps that knew the caverns,
I know the soft morning huddle of my body,
the lead weight swing of getting from
one measurement of chronology to the next,
crawling along, either end of the tunnel
opening like a sigh.

Past Forty

What point have I come to, being past forty,
when after an ordinary supper,
someone else bent under the kitchen light
doing inevitable dishes,
I allow the turning hour to take me,
compelling me to wander among quiet deer
grazing close-clipped autumn lawns?

In the orchard, I collect windfalls
for those same deer, speak sadly
to the foolish plum,
blooming in September,
porcupine-pruned in May,
count the pumpkins waiting for illumination,
as am I, as am I.

After the repetition of the seasons,
I know each page of this evening book,
understand that which is common—
the deer, shadows in tangled firs and vine maple by day,
appearing each evening,
sudden statuary in the fading light—
have charted the changes,
the plague of porcupines,
the millennium of apples after a cold winter,

yet cannot put the book aside.
Returning, I light a first protecting fire
and accept that I must do all this,
this strolling of the evening gallery,
these acts of husbandry,
knowing no barrier between myself
and what I care for
at this point past forty.

The Breathing Lesson

The woman who lives alone decides on a day of silence,
then notices how often she forgets to breathe
and is more alone.
She hears the clock tick,
the windchime speak to its wind,
hears rain leave and return to the roof,
learns the clock of her body.
Now every space fills with breathing.

But by noon all facts are forgotten.
That contents her.
She eats silence for lunch,
sees the firs breathing outside,
bearing at last, fruited with gravity.
Gravity can be movement, she believes it,
can be a pause, one she can touch.
The more she is silent,
the heavier the branches become.
Knowing nothing at all by nightfall,
she stitches a blue cape, a windcatcher.
Ready for the road out, she steps over the faded sign
facedown in the dust.

Acknowledgments

Thank you to all who have encouraged my poetry over the years, in particular Erik Muller of *Fireweed* magazine and Traprock Press. Harold L. Johnson, beloved friend, has given me kind readings and multiple, wide-ranging coffee shop conversations for many years now. Marvin Bell, David Lee, and Naomi Shihab Nye were inspiring teachers. Paulann Petersen, former Oregon State Poet Laureate, welcomed me to Portland by including me in readings and workshops.

In memory and gratitude to my lifelong friend and once husband, the late Douglas Getchell, who first believed in my poetry.

My thanks to the following magazines and their editors for first publishing the following poems:

The Beacon: "Postcard from a Family Reunion," "That Winter," "Raids on Afghanistan"
Calapooya Collage: "For Donald"
Calyx: "Arithmetic"
Convolvulus: "Weather"
Fireweed: Poetry of Western Oregon: "In the Lane," "Matins," "Our First Words Each Day," "What Do I Know?"
Thema: "Reflection: The Annual Visit"

"Weather People" received a Poet's Choice Award from Oregon Poetry Association.
"A Country and Western Song" was written from a workshop assignment by poet Marvin Bell.

Biography

Stephanie Van Horn was born in a New Jersey farm community, home to her family for many generations. In 1959 she, her younger brother, and her parents relocated to Southern California. She graduated with a degree in English from UCLA and has graduate degrees in English and education. Oregon has been her home since 1983. She taught for thirty-three years in various settings, with the last fifteen years spent as a professor of English at Southwestern Oregon Community College. After retirement and a move to Portland, she has been songwriting and performing and is currently completing a novel.

www.ingramcontent.com/pod-product-compliance
Lightning Source LLC
Chambersburg PA
CBHW021953290426
44108CB00012B/1051